Roald Dahl's

The Three Little

Pigs

a tail-twistingly treacherous musical

by **Matthew White** and **Ana Sanderson**
with orchestral music by **Paul Patterson**

A & C Black
in association with The Roald Dahl Foundation and Music Link International

CUE:

(Use this space to write your own reminder of the action which precedes the song)

SINGERS:

PIG ONE
PIG TWO
PIG THREE
GROUPS 1, 2 AND 3

Snouts and curly tails

Declamatory ♩ = 120

ALL: *f*

Now lis - ten, ev - 'ry - bo - dy! It's time to pay at - ten - tion, And just be - fore we start the show, There's some - thing we should men - tion. We'd like a bit of qui - et, please, We'd

al - so like ap - plause, We don't want groans or mo - bile phones, Or fid - get - ing or snores. Now

sit up straight and con - cen - trate, We'd like you all to meet A por - ky lit - tle tri - o, Who have

snouts and cur - ly tails and lit - tle trot - ters In - stead of feet!

Vs.1 GROUPS 2 and 3:
Vs.2 GROUPS 1 and 3:

Vs.1 Pig One was round and fat, He had a
(Vs.2) Two was ve - ry dif - f'rent, He was

some-times made him sigh,
gave him cause to fear,
Was the ti-ni-est sus-pi-cion, Just the tee-ni-est sus-pi-cion, Yes, the

Chorus
ALL:

wee-ni-est sus-pi-cion That he'd end up in a pie!
That a wolf was lurk-ing near!
Let's

hear it for the pig! P. I. G. 'Cos that's the sort of a-ni-mal we'd like to

1.

GROUPS 1 and 3:

be.

Vs.2 Pig

Wolf coming!

With an air of suspense ♩. = 60

ALL (EXCEPT WOLF):

Eyes glint-ing, Twigs crack-ling,

Fur brist-ling, Wolf... com-ing! Wolf... com-ing,

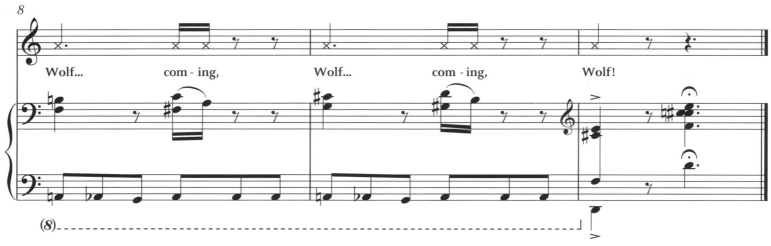

Wolf... com-ing, Wolf... com-ing, Wolf!

Huff and puff 1

Getting louder and faster throughout ♩. = 70

I'll huff and I'll puff and I'll blow your house in, I'll huff and I'll puff and I'll blow your house in, I'll huff and I'll puff and I'll blow your house in!

accel.

(The house is blown down.)

Blowing sound effects

sub. *p* cresc.

Never-ending appetite

With a swing ♩. = 120

ALL (EXCEPT WOLF):

Did-n't you hear a squeal? Did-n't you hear a squelch? A

crack - ling and a___ slurp?___ *(slurp)* Did-n't you hear a gasp?

17 Wolf is on the loose and he's ap-proach-ing___ us!___

19 *Chorus* Well I ne - ver! What a cu - ri - ous sight,___ A

21 hun-gry wolf and a ne - ver - end - ing ap - pe-tite! He's a bul - ly, he's a

24 ra - ve-nous beast!_ But he saves a lit - tle some-thing from his tas - ty___ feast._

Roald Dahl's
The Three Little Pigs

Script

Contents

A & C Black

in association with The Roald Dahl Foundation and Music Link International

INTRODUCTION

This musical version of **The Three Little Pigs** is based on one of the poems from Roald Dahl's much-loved collection of **Revolting Rhymes**. In addition to the poem, this adaptation includes songs and opportunities for dance. There are also orchestral excerpts included on the CD; these are taken from Paul Patterson's commissioned orchestral work, also inspired by this *Revolting Rhyme*. Various excerpts from this work can be incorporated into your performance to accompany mime, movement and scene changes. Many of the songs in this musical also contain themes and ideas from the orchestral work.

The Three Little Pigs is designed to be as flexible as possible so that, whatever your resources, you can stage a successful production. Whether you are aiming for something large and impressive, or small-scale and simple, you will need a clear plan to help you get the best results. For this purpose we have provided a Production Overview (see pages 4–5).

Who's in charge?

Professional musical theatre productions will employ a director, a musical director, a designer, a lighting designer and often a choreographer. Consider what you can do yourself and what you can delegate to others. For example, you may have some talented parents who will actively enjoy helping out with the set, costumes or props. The children themselves may be able to take on some of the production responsibilities – they can contribute in all sorts of ways, both on stage and off.

Real instruments or backing tracks?

You (or your musical director) will need to decide which CD tracks you want to use in rehearsal and performance. The accompanying CD includes backing tracks and vocal performances of all the songs to help you in rehearsal. You will also need to decide whether to use the backing tracks in performance, or whether to have live piano accompaniment, or even clarinet and bassoon (instrumental parts are provided on the CD-ROM).

If you are using the CD at any point in your performance, you will need to appoint someone reliable to be in charge of the CD player.

Listen to the CD as you read through the script and devise a plan to suit you and your specific requirements. Be prepared to be flexible – do not worry if you cannot include every suggestion, or even every song, in the show. Mix and match to suit your circumstances.

Performing the show

To involve as many children as possible, it is suggested you have group singing, unless you have particularly confident singers. The chorus is divided into three singing groups:

Group 1: Farm animals who can sing with Pig One.

Group 2: Woodland animals who can sing with Pig Two.

Group 3: City types (animals or humans) who can sing with Pig Three.

There are several useful points to remember when performing a show:

- *Confident delivery and clarity*: encourage the children to project their voices, to avoid rushing the poetry or dialogue, and, where possible, to face the audience when speaking and singing.

- *Understanding the text*: make sure that the children understand exactly what they are singing or saying. It may not always be obvious to them whether or not their lines are supposed to be funny.

- *Character*: often when young performers are working with poetry, they sacrifice everything to the rhythm of the rhyme. The results can be a bit lifeless and uninspired. It is more important to remember the character that is being played; most of the time the rhyme will take care of itself.

There are acting games on the CD-ROM to help develop these aspects of the performance.

What are the staging requirements?

Nobody knows the circumstances of your particular production better than you do and you should feel free to interpret the piece in any way you feel is appropriate.

The most important consideration, if there are lots of children involved, is space. Think carefully about your performance space whether it is an area with rostra blocks or a permanent raised platform. Consider how you will get children on and off the stage. If you are intending to use large numbers of children for your performance, you may want to avoid too much moving about during the show. If, as suggested, you are intending to use three groups of singers, you may want to position them at the start of the show and then leave them where they are. Make sure there are clear routes to and from the performance area and try to have a clear pathway through the audience, if possible, for the entrance of the Wolf.

If you are using live instruments, you will need space for the piano and any other instruments you are including. Do the children need to see the pianist for musical cues?

Where scenery is concerned, don't be afraid to appeal to the imagination of the audience. Props and costumes can be effective scene setters. Keeping scenery to a minimum will allow scene changes to be carried out swiftly and without disturbing the dramatic flow of the show. There are some simple staging ideas on page 6, and further suggestions on the CD-ROM. Remember these are only suggestions – you and the children will have equally valid ideas.

CAST LIST

All the characters in this piece can be played by girls or boys. The three Pigs are referred to as male, as this is how they are presented in Dahl's poem. Obviously, you can change this to suit your casting needs.

PIG ONE
Pig One is rotund – he is probably being fattened up for eating! He has three lines of poetry and should be able to 'oink' very convincingly! He also has some lines to chant, which can be doubled by Group 1.

PIG TWO
Pig Two is sporty and energetic; he is always upbeat and positive. He has five lines of poetry. He also has some lines to chant, which can be doubled by Group 2.

PIG THREE
Pig Three is a bigger role than the other two Pigs. He is cocky and confident and has fourteen lines of poetry. If he is a confident singer, he might sing solo in 'Wheeler-dealer piggy'.

WOLF
Wolf is sly, boastful and always hungry. The child playing this role should be confident and enjoy the challenge of scaring the audience. Wolf has eighteen lines of poetry and some solo chanted lines in the three 'Huff and puff' chants and in 'Never-ending appetite', if desired.

RED RIDING HOOD
Red Riding Hood is strong-willed and blood-thirsty, although she makes a show of being sweet and lovable. She has ten lines of poetry and if she is a confident singer, she could sing the two verses of 'Perfectly marvellous me!' as solos.

PHOTOGRAPHER
The photographer appears briefly in the final scene, so he or she should be played by a member of the general chorus. He or she has no solo lines to speak or sing.

CHORUS
Each of the three Pigs can be supported by a specific, easily identifiable group. Pig One has a group of Farm animals, Pig Two has a group of Woodland animals, and Pig Three has a group of City types (who could be either humans or animals). You can decide what kind of animals or specific characters you want them to be.

Some members of the chorus have solo spoken lines of poetry. Do not feel bound to follow the allocation of these lines in the script to the letter – divide them up amongst the chorus members to suit your circumstances.

The chorus can take on all of the singing in this show, if desired, or the singing can be divided up between chorus groups and soloists.

3

PRODUCTION OVERVIEW

SCENE 1

THE WOODLAND: The three little Pigs are introduced and we hear that there is a wolf on the prowl.

ON STAGE: PIG ONE
PIG TWO
PIG THREE
CHORUS:
FARM ANIMALS
WOODLAND ANIMALS
CITY TYPES

PROPS: MOBILE PHONE

1 **OVERTURE**
(during which the audience is seated)

2 **SONG**
Snouts and curly tails

SCRIPT

SCENE 2

THE HOUSE OF STRAW: Pig One builds his house of straw. Wolf blows the house down and eats him.

ON STAGE: PIG ONE
WOLF
CHORUS:
FARM ANIMALS
WOODLAND ANIMALS
CITY TYPES

PROPS: PIG'S CURLY TAIL

3 **MUSIC**
Building the house of straw

4 **CHANT**
Wolf coming!

SCRIPT

5 **CHANT**
Huff and puff 1

SCRIPT

6 **MUSIC**
Wolf chases Pig One

SCRIPT

7 **SONG**
Never-ending appetite

SCRIPT

SCENE 3

THE HOUSE OF TWIGS: Pig Two builds the house of twigs. Wolf blows the house down and eats him.

ON STAGE: PIG TWO
WOLF
CHORUS:
FARM ANIMALS
WOODLAND ANIMALS
CITY TYPES

PROPS: PIG'S CURLY TAIL

8 **MUSIC**
Building the house of twigs

SCRIPT

9 **CHANT**
Huff and puff 2

SCRIPT

10 **MUSIC**
Wolf chases Pig Two

SCRIPT

11 **SONG**
Never-ending appetite (reprise)

SCRIPT

SCENE 4

THE HOUSE OF BRICKS: Pig Three builds his house of bricks. Wolf tries to blow the house down, but fails. He decides to blow the house up instead. Pig Three rings up Red Riding Hood for help.

ON STAGE: PIG THREE
WOLF
CHORUS:
FARM ANIMALS
WOODLAND ANIMALS
CITY TYPES

PROPS: MOBILE PHONE

12 **MUSIC**
Building the house of bricks

13 **SONG**
Wheeler-dealer piggy

SCRIPT

14 **CHANT**
Huff and puff 3

SCRIPT

15 **SCENE CHANGE**

SCENE 5

RED RIDING HOOD'S HOUSE: Red Riding Hood tells Pig Three that she will come over to help as soon as she has finished washing her hair.

ON STAGE: RED RIDING HOOD
PIG THREE
CHORUS:
FARM ANIMALS
WOODLAND ANIMALS
CITY TYPES

PROPS: TELEPHONE
DRESSING TABLE
CHAIR
MIRROR
HAIR BRUSH
HAIR DRYER

16 **SOUND EFFECT**
Telephone ring

SCRIPT

17 **SONG**
Perfectly marvellous me!

18 **SCENE CHANGE**

SCENE 6

THE WOODLAND: Red Riding Hood appears and shoots Wolf dead. Everybody celebrates and Red Riding Hood and Pig Three exit hand-in-trotter. A gunshot is heard. Red Riding Hood reappears with a pigskin travelling case.

ON STAGE: RED RIDING HOOD
PIG THREE
WOLF
PHOTOGRAPHER
CHORUS:
FARM ANIMALS
WOODLAND ANIMALS
CITY TYPES

PROPS: COMIC PISTOL
CAMERA
PIGSKIN TRAVELLING CASE

SCRIPT

19 **SOUND EFFECT**
Gunshot

20 **CHANT**
Wolf dying

SCRIPT

21 **SONG**
Done and dusted

22 **SOUND EFFECT**
Gunshot

SCRIPT

23 **SONG**
Finale

5

STAGING SUGGESTIONS

The Three Little Pigs is presented in six scenes. However, the entire musical could be performed against a woodland backdrop eg:

Scene 1: a woodland backdrop, eg a simple painted backcloth depicting trees and foliage.

Scenes 2-4: a woodland backdrop with houses of straw, twigs and bricks in the foreground as appropriate. (See below for ideas on how to represent the houses.)

Scene 5: the woodland backdrop remains but add simple props to suggest that this is inside Red Riding Hood's house: a chair for her to sit in, a dressing table with a telephone and a mirror.

Scene 6: woodland backdrop.

Any scene changes should be simple and quick to perform. Orchestral extracts are provided on the CD to accompany scene changes to allow props to be brought on and off the stage.

Building and blowing down the houses

Here are some simple suggestions for how to present the construction and destruction of the house of straw and the house of twigs, and the construction of the house of bricks, which Wolf fails to blow down. You and the children may well find different and better ways or you may like to mix, match and adapt some of the following ideas.

However you choose to construct the houses, the orchestral extracts on the CD are there to accompany the action.

Suggestion 1 – cardboard boxes

Use a large cardboard box, painted to look like it is made of straw, twigs, bricks etc. For the straw and twig house, real straw and twigs could be stuck on to the outside.

The Pigs do not necessarily have to be inside the house – they could be standing on one side, whilst the Wolf stands on the other. Or the Pigs could stand behind the house, so their heads poke up over the roof. The chorus (Farm animals for the house of straw, Woodland animals for the house of twigs and City types for the house of bricks) could carry the houses onto the stage.

Suggestion 2 – bamboo pole and cloth hanging

Take a length of bamboo and hang a large piece of cloth (eg a sheet cut to size) over it – imagine a table cloth or sheet hanging on a washing line. The cloth can be painted and decorated to look like a house of straw, twigs or bricks.

Again, the Pigs can stand to one side of the house or behind, their heads peeping nervously over the top. Two members of the chorus (eg Farm animals for the house of straw etc) could carry the houses on and off the stage.

Suggestion 3 – dance

This is a more abstract method of presenting the houses. For the straw house, for example, give the Farm animals poles decorated with straw to hold and create a dance/movement sequence which finishes with the Farm animals positioned in a circle (possibly crouching or kneeling) around Pig One (see illustration below).

To form Pig Two's house, use large twigs or small branches. For the house of bricks, each child could carry a short pole with a 'brick' on the end, eg made from a shoe-box and painted. Remember that the children forming the house of bricks will need to remain in position for some time, so they must be able to rest their props easily.

Blowing down the houses

The blowing down of the houses of straw and twigs are accompanied by the *Huff and puff* chants. Remember that the house of bricks is not blown down and should not be taken off until the end of Scene 5.

Chasing and eating Pig One and Pig Two

Orchestral extracts are provided on the CD to use as an accompaniment to the chase sequences. Think carefully about how they will be staged. Could Pig One and Pig Two run into the audience and hide behind a spectator? Could it involve a circuit of the school hall? You might like to have at least one spare pig's curly tail (see Costume suggestions) so that the Pig's tail does not need to be ripped off his costume off-stage after the chase and so Wolf can appear brandishing it afterwards.

Pig One and Pig Two could be eaten to an accompaniment of blood-curdling sounds made by the children (as exaggerated as they like). These could be performed live or pre-recorded.

Death of the Wolf

Red Riding Hood's pistol should be a comic-style gun and should not look in any way realistic. 'Drawing a pistol from her knickers' may be difficult to achieve on stage – it might be better for her to have the pistol in her upstage hand (furthest from the audience) when she enters. Make sure that the Wolf dies as close to the side of the stage as possible, however protracted his death, so that he can leave the stage easily.

COSTUME IDEAS

Roald Dahl wrote the poem with a contemporary setting, eg Red Riding Hood talks to Pig Three on the phone, and this musical adaptation also contains contemporary references, eg the City types. Therefore, it may be best to set your production in contemporary times too and the costumes should reflect this. (If you choose to present the show as a 'period piece', be aware that there will be one or two anachronisms!)

Most of the characters in this piece are animals and you may wish to present these using masks or head-dresses. Avoid designs which obscure the children's features, especially their eyes, since children's faces are full of expression and life and will enhance any performance. Animal characters are always better presented on two legs, rather than four. They will be able to project their voices more effectively if their faces are not directed towards the floor.

THE THREE LITTLE PIGS
For each of the three little Pigs, make a curly pink tail by plaiting together some strips of material and weaving in some wire to enable the tail to be twisted into shape. You could attach the tail to the seat of their trousers or tops. Ears can either be attached to a hooded top, or secured onto the head with elastic (or onto an Alice band). Piggy snouts could be made out of an egg carton or even a small paper cup, which could be attached to some elastic or string and looped around the back of the head.

PIG ONE
Pig One's costume will need a fair amount of padding. You could use an adult-sized hooded top, or sweatshirt (preferably pink or red), and stuff it with odd bits of material (or even screwed up newspaper) until it is bulging at the seams. He could also wear an old pair of dirty dungarees over the top.

PIG TWO
Pig Two should probably be dressed in some sort of tracksuit, or maybe a football strip (pink or red would be ideal, if you can find it!). To emphasise his sporty image, he could perhaps wear a baseball cap with piggy ears attached. He could also carry a Walkman or Ipod with headphones so that he can listen to music as he jogs along.

PIG THREE
Pig Three should look slightly more formal than the other Pigs, perhaps with a jacket, shirt and tie (again, pink or red is ideal). He could be carrying a mobile phone in his pocket and could also carry a laptop.

WOLF
You may want to make a wolf costume out of synthetic fur, which, if you have the time and expertise can be very effective. A similar effect can be achieved much more simply, however, by using a fake fur coat. A tail can be made out of a length of rope (you could cover it with fur or simply paint it the same colour as the fur coat). Ears can be attached to the child's head with an Alice band, a piece of elastic, or a ring of card. You could also give Wolf some furry spats which would give the impression of big furry feet. If you want him to be a bit more scary, you could also create claws by using false finger-nails or by fitting specially-made claws to a pair of gloves.

RED RIDING HOOD
The most important thing about Red Riding Hood is that she is very vain, so whatever you decide to dress her in, she should look as though she has made an effort. Even though she ultimately puts on a fur coat towards the end of her song *Perfectly marvellous me!*, it is a good idea to put her in a red cape or cloak from the beginning of Scene 5 to establish her character.

PHOTOGRAPHER
He/she needs a camera as a prop.

FARM AND WOODLAND ANIMALS
Lots of fun can be had with the animal costumes. Hats or headpieces incorporating obvious animal characteristics such as ears, snouts and manes can be very effective. To keep it simple, concentrate on the headpieces and tails – the rest of the costume can just be a simple T-shirt and trousers/tights in a suitable colour (yellow for a hen, brown for a pony, grey for a rabbit etc).

CITY TYPES
If your City types are animals, give them a suitable mask or head-dress and tail and dress them in shirts, ties and jackets. Alternatively, if your group of City types are human, then give them a clear city look, eg smart skirts and jackets for the girls, shirts and ties for the boys.

7

The script

OVERTURE

This may be played as the audience is seated.

Fade when ready

SCENE 1 - The woodland

The performers enter and position themselves ready for the performance.

SONG – Snouts and curly tails

ALL
> Now listen, ev'rybody,
> It's time to pay attention,
> And just before we start the show,
> There's something we should mention.
> We'd like a bit of quiet, please,
> We'd also like applause,
> We don't want groans or mobile phones,
> Or fidgeting or snores.
> Now sit up straight and concentrate,
> We'd like you all to meet
> A porky little trio,
> Who have snouts and curly tails and little trotters
> Instead of feet!

Verse 1

GROUPS 2 AND 3
> Pig One was round and fat,
> He had a barrel for a belly.

Pig One appears; he is very plump and moves slowly.

PIG 1 AND GROUP 1   *(chanted)* Oink! Oink! Oink! Oink! Squelch!

GROUPS 2 AND 3
> He lived down on a farm
> And was ridiculously smelly!

PIG 1 AND GROUP 1   *(chanted)* Oink! Oink! Oink! Oink! Squelch!

8

| GROUPS 2 AND 3 | One thing, though, that worried him,
That sometimes made him sigh,
Was the tiniest suspicion,
Just the teeniest suspicion,
Yes, the weeniest suspicion
That he'd end up in a pie! |

Chorus

| ALL | Let's hear it for the pig!
P.I.G.
'Cos that's the sort of animal we'd like to be. |

Verse 2

| GROUPS 1 AND 3 | Pig Two was very diff'rent,
He was sporty and athletic. |

Pig Two appears, jogging; he is very fit and energetic.

PIG 2 AND GROUP 2	*(chanted)* Hup, 2, 3 and 4 and hup, 2, 3 and 4!
GROUPS 1 AND 3	He lived down in the forest And was keen and energetic.
PIG 2 AND GROUP 2	*(chanted)* Hup, 2, 3 and 4 and hup, 2, 3 and 4!
GROUPS 1 AND 3	One thing, though, that worried him, That gave him cause to fear, Was the tiniest suspicion, Just the teeniest suspicion, Yes, the weeniest suspicion That a wolf was lurking near!

Chorus

| ALL | Let's hear it for the pig!
P.I.G.
'Cos that's the sort of animal we'd like to be. |

Verse 3

| GROUPS 1 AND 2 | Pig Three was so ambitious,
He knew just where he was going. |

Pig Three appears; he is dressed as a city trader and carries a mobile phone.

PIG 3 AND GROUP 3	*(chanted)* Speculate, accumulate, buy and sell!
GROUPS 1 AND 2	He worked down in the city And his bank account was growing!
PIG 3 AND GROUP 3	*(chanted)* Speculate, accumulate, buy and sell!
GROUPS 1 AND 2	One thing, though, that worried him, That made him want to sob, Was the tiniest suspicion, Just the teeniest suspicion, Yes, the weeniest suspicion That he'd one day lose his job!

9

Chorus

ALL	Let's hear it for the pig!
	P.I.G.
	'Cos that's the sort of animal we'd like to be.

The three groups chant their sections together:

PIG 1 AND GROUP 1	**Oink! Oink! Oink! Oink! Squelch!**
	Oink! Oink! Oink! Oink! Squelch! *(continue)*
PIG 2 AND GROUP 2	**Hup, 2, 3 and 4 and hup, 2, 3 and 4!**
	Hup, 2, 3 and 4 and hup, 2, 3 and 4! *(continue)*
PIG 3 AND GROUP 3	**Speculate, accumulate, buy and sell!**
	Speculate, accumulate, buy and sell! *(everybody finishes)*

ALL	Let's hear it for the pig!
	P.I.G.
	'Cos that's the sort of animal we'd like to be.
	He's our inspiration,
	He'll never fail,
	With a snout, four little trotters
	And a curly tail!

Forward to next track

(APPLAUSE)

PIG 1	The animal I really dig
	Above all others is the pig.
PIG 2	Pigs are noble!
PIG 3	Pigs are clever!
PIGS 1, 2 AND 3	Pigs are courteous ...
FARM ANIMAL 1	However,
	Now and then, to break this rule,
	One meets a pig who is a fool.

Everyone looks at Pig One.

FARM ANIMAL 2	What, for example, would you say
	If strolling through the woods one day,
	Right there in front of you you saw
FARM ANIMALS 1, 2 AND 3	A pig who'd built his house of STRAW!

10

SCENE 2 – The house of straw

 MUSIC – Building the house of straw

Pig One and Group 1 build the house of straw (see page 6 in this pull-out section for suggestions on how to stage this). The children could also compose their own music to accompany the action – see CD-ROM Music Activity. By the end of the music, the house of straw should be in position.

 CHANT – Wolf coming!

As the children perform the chant, Wolf appears, perhaps through the audience.

ALL (EXCEPT WOLF)	**Eyes glinting,**
	Twigs crackling,
	Fur bristling,
	Wolf ... coming!
	Eyes glinting,
	Twigs crackling,
	Fur bristling,
	Wolf ... coming,
	Wolf ... coming,
	Wolf ... coming,
	Wolf!
FARM ANIMAL 1	The wolf appeared and licked his lips,
	And said ...
WOLF	That pig has had his chips.
	Little pig, little pig, let me come in!
PIG 1	No, no, by the hairs on my chinny-chin-chin!
WOLF	Then I'll huff and I'll puff and I'll blow your house in!
FARM ANIMAL 2	The little pig began to pray,
	But Wolfie blew his house away.

Forward to next track

 CHANT – Huff and puff 1

Everyone performs the chant, getting louder throughout. They then make sound effects for Wolf blowing down the house of straw (see CD-ROM Music Activity). On the final chord, the house is blown down (see CD-ROM Music Activity for ideas on creating sound effects).

WOLF AND ALL	**I'll huff and I'll puff and I'll blow your house in,**
	I'll huff and I'll puff and I'll blow your house in,
	I'll huff and I'll puff and I'll blow your house in!
	(Blowing sound effects)
	(Final chord: the house is blown down)

Forward to next track

The house is taken off-stage and Pig One is left stranded.

11

FARM ANIMAL 3	Wolf shouted ...
WOLF	Bacon, pork and ham! Oh, what a lucky Wolf I am!

MUSIC – Wolf chases Pig One

Wolf chases Pig One around the stage until they exit into the wings or behind a tree (see Staging Suggestions on page 6 of this pull-out section). Screeches and squelches are heard from off-stage, as the Pig is gobbled up. Wolf then appears back on stage brandishing Pig One's curly tail.

FARM ANIMAL 1	And though he ate the pig quite fast ...
FARM ANIMALS 1, 2 AND 3	He carefully kept the tail till last.

SONG – Never-ending appetite

Verse 1

ALL (EXCEPT WOLF)
Didn't you hear a squeal?
Didn't you hear a squelch?
A crackling and a slurp? *(slurp)*
Didn't you hear a gasp?
Didn't you hear a groan?
And one enormous burp? *(burp)*
Wolf has had his picnic here
And look, he's saved a curly little souvenir!

Wolf holds up Pig One's tail.

Didn't you hear the news?
Didn't you hear the fuss?
A wolf is on the loose and he's approaching us!

Chorus
Well I never! What a curious sight,
A hungry wolf and a never-ending appetite!
He's a bully, he's a ravenous beast!
But he saves a little something from his tasty feast.

Chant

GROUPS 1, 2 AND 3	What if you ate a goat?
WOLF	I'd save his coat!
GROUPS 1, 2 AND 3	What if you ate a whale?
WOLF	I'd save his tail!

12

GROUPS 1, 2 AND 3	Elephant?
WOLF	Trunk!
GROUPS 1, 2 AND 3	Butterfly?
WOLF	Wing!
GROUPS 1, 2 AND 3	Hummingbird?
WOLF	Hum!
GROUPS 1, 2 AND 3	Jellyfish?
WOLF	Sting!
ALL	There's always something to savour from just about anything!

Chorus

ALL (EXCEPT WOLF) Well I never! What a curious sight,
A hungry wolf and a never-ending appetite!
He's a bully, he's a ravenous beast!
But he saves a little something,
A tempting little something ...
A tantalising something from his tasty feast.

(APPLAUSE)

Forward to next track

Wolf holds up Pig One's tail and begins to chew on it as the narration continues.

WOODLAND ANIMAL 1 Wolf wandered on, a trifle bloated.
Surprise, surprise, for soon he noted
Another little house for pigs ...

WOODLAND
ANIMALS 1, 2 AND 3 And this one had been built of TWIGS!

Wolf stands to one side and watches as the house of twigs is built.

13

SCENE 3 – The house of twigs

Forward to
next track

MUSIC – Building the house of twigs

Pig Two and Group 2 build the house of twigs (see page 6 in this pull-out section for suggestions on how to stage this). The children could also compose their own music to accompany the action – see CD-ROM Music Activity.

WOLF   Little pig, little pig, let me come in!

PIG 2   No, no, by the hairs on my chinny-chin-chin!

WOLF   Then I'll huff and I'll puff and I'll blow your house in!

WOODLAND
ANIMAL 2   The Wolf said ...

WOLF   Okay, here we go!

WOODLAND
ANIMAL 2   He then began to blow and blow.

CHANT – Huff and puff 2

Everyone performs the chant, getting louder throughout. They then make sound effects for Wolf blowing down the house of twigs (see CD-ROM Music Activity). On the final chord, the house is blown down (see CD-ROM Music Activity for ideas on creating sound effects).

WOLF AND ALL   **I'll huff and I'll puff and I'll blow your house in,**
                      I'll huff and I'll puff and I'll blow your house in,
                      I'll huff and I'll puff and I'll blow your house in!

                      (Blowing sound effects)
                      (Final chord: the house is blown down)

Forward to
next track

The house is taken off-stage and Pig Two is left stranded.

WOODLAND
ANIMAL 3   The little pig began to squeal.
                      He cried ...

PIG 2   Oh Wolf, you've had one meal!
                      Why can't we talk and make a deal?

WOODLAND
ANIMAL 1   The Wolf replied ...

WOLF   Not on your nelly!

WOODLAND
ANIMAL 1   And soon the pig was in his belly.

14

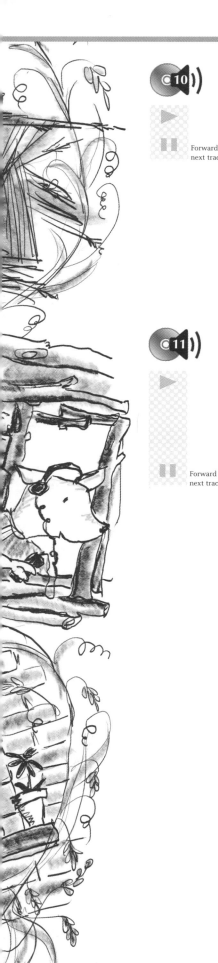

Forward to next track

MUSIC – Wolf chases Pig Two

Wolf chases Pig Two around the stage until they exit into the wings (see Staging Suggestions on page 6 of this pull-out section). More screeches and squelches are heard from off-stage, as Pig Two is gobbled up. Wolf then appears back on stage waving Pig Two's curly tail.

WOLF	Two juicy little pigs!
WOODLAND ANIMAL 2	Wolf cried ...
WOLF	But still I am not satisfied! I know full well my tummy's bulging, But oh, how I adore indulging.

Forward to next track

SONG – Never-ending appetite (reprise)

Chorus

ALL (EXCEPT WOLF)	Well I never! What a curious sight, A hungry wolf and a never-ending appetite! He's a bully, he's a ravenous beast! But he saves a little something, A tempting little something ... A tantalising something from his tasty feast.

Wolf holds up Pig Two's tail and begins to chew on it as the narration continues.

CITY TYPE 1	So, creeping quietly as a mouse, The Wolf approached another house ...
CITY TYPE 2	A house which also had inside A little piggy trying to hide.
PIG 3	But this one, Piggy Number Three, Was bright and brainy as could be!
CITY TYPE 3	No straw for him, no twigs or sticks.
CITY TYPES 1, 2 AND 3	This pig had built his house of BRICKS.

Wolf stands to one side and watches as the house of bricks is built.

Scene 4 – The house of bricks

  MUSIC – Building the house of bricks

Pig Three and Group 3 build the house of bricks (see page 6 in this pull-out section for suggestions on how to stage this). The children could also compose their own music to accompany the action – see CD-ROM Music Activity.

 SONG – Wheeler-dealer piggy

Introduction

ALL *(clap, clap)*
(clap, clap)

Verse 1

PIG 3 AND GROUP 3 When I was just a little pig,
I told myself when I grew big,
That I would quit my smelly sty,
And change my life by aiming high.
And so I strove to get ahead,
I would've sold my granny if she wasn't dead.
And now there's none but me to thank,
I've got a load of lolly in my piggy bank!

Chorus

I'm a wheeler-dealer piggy!
GROUPS 1 AND 2 (A wheeler-dealer piggy!)
PIG 3 AND GROUP 3 With talent, charisma and flair.
I'm a wheeler-dealer piggy!
GROUPS 1 AND 2 (A wheeler-dealer piggy!)
PIG 3 AND GROUP 3 A self-made, money-making millionaire!
So watch this space,
Get out of my face,
What you get is what you see!
'Cos I'm a wheeler-dealer piggy!
GROUPS 1 AND 2 (A wheeler-dealer piggy!)
PIG 3 AND GROUP 3 A wheeler-dealer pig, that's me!
(clap, clap)
(clap, clap)

Verse 2

PIG 3 AND GROUP 3 I started life with nothing much
But now I've got the Midas touch;
I've got a yacht, I've got a plane,
A house in France and one in Spain.
I even built this house of brick,
It's not a thing of beauty but the walls are thick!
And any wolf with any sense
Would try to keep away from my electric fence!

16

Chorus

	I'm a wheeler-dealer piggy!
GROUPS 1 AND 2	(A wheeler-dealer piggy!)
PIG 3 AND GROUP 3	With talent, charisma and flair.
	I'm a wheeler-dealer piggy!
GROUPS 1 AND 2	(A wheeler-dealer piggy!)
PIG 3 AND GROUP 3	A self-made, money-making millionaire!
	So watch this space,
	Get out of my face,
	What you get is what you see!
	'Cos I'm a wheeler-dealer piggy!
GROUPS 1 AND 2	(A wheeler-dealer piggy!)
PIG 3 AND GROUP 3	A wheeler-dealer pig, that's me!
ALL	*(clap, clap)*
	(clap, clap)
	A wheeler-dealer pig, that's me!

 Forward to next track

(APPLAUSE)

PIG 3	You'll not get me!
CITY TYPE 1	The Piggy cried.
WOLF	I'll blow you down!
CITY TYPE 1	The Wolf replied.
PIG 3	You're going to need a lot of puff,
	And I don't think you've got enough.
CITY TYPE 2	Wolf huffed and puffed and blew and blew.
	The house stayed up as good as new.

CHANT – Huff and puff 3

Everyone performs the chant, getting louder and louder throughout. They then make sound effects for Wolf trying to blow down the house of bricks (see CD-ROM Music Activity).

WOLF AND ALL	I'll huff and I'll puff and I'll blow your house in,
	I'll huff and I'll puff and I'll blow your house in,
	I'll huff and I'll puff and I'll blow your house in!

(Blowing sound effects)

Forward to next track

Wolf, defeated, stops blowing.

| WOLF | If I can't blow it down ... |
| CITY TYPE 3 | Wolf said ... |

17

WOLF	I'll have to blow it up instead. I'll come back in the dead of night And blow it up with dynamite!
CITY TYPE 2	Pig cried ...
PIG 3	You brute! I might have known!
CITY TYPE 2	Then, picking up the telephone, He dialled as quickly as he could The number of Miss Riding Hood.

SCENE CHANGE

Props are brought on to set the scene for Red Riding Hood's house. Red Riding Hood enters, sits down at the dressing table and starts to brush her hair, gazing admiringly at herself in the mirror. The children could also compose their own music here to accompany the scene change – see CD-ROM Music Activity.

SCENE 5 - Red Riding Hood's house

SOUND EFFECT – Telephone

The phone rings. Red Riding Hood breaks off from brushing her hair and picks up the phone.

RED RIDING HOOD	Hello?...hello? Who's speaking? Who? Oh, hello Piggy, how d'you do?
PIG 3	I really need your help, Miss Hood! Oh help me, please! D'you think you could?
RED RIDING HOOD	I'll try, of course ...
WOODLAND ANIMAL 1	Miss Hood replied.
RED RIDING HOOD	What's on your mind?
PIG 3	A Wolf ... outside! I know you've dealt with wolves before, And now I've got one at my door!
RED RIDING HOOD	My darling Pig, my precious sweet, That's something really up my street. I've just begun to wash my hair. But when it's dry, I'll be right there.

 18

SONG – Perfectly marvellous me!

Red Riding Hood is combing her hair and staring into a mirror. She sings the verses either as a solo, or with one of the three chorus groups.

Verse 1

RED RIDING HOOD
Look in the mirror,
What do I see?
Little me!
Gorgeous and lovable,
Curls in my hair,
As cute as can be,
Perfectly marvellous me!

ALL (EXCEPT RRH)   BUT!

Chorus

Never judge a book by its cover!
Little girls have stories to tell.
You may think she's like any other,
Brother, you don't know her too well.
Stay awake! Stay aware!
If she's coming your way, head south!
She'll try to pretend
That she's your life-long friend
And butter won't melt in her mouth!

Red Riding Hood puts on her wolfskin coat.

Verse 2

RED RIDING HOOD
Look in the mirror,
What do I see?
Little me!
Quite irresistible!
Sunny and sweet
And kind as can be ...
Perfectly marvellous me!

ALL (EXCEPT RRH)   BUT!

Chorus

Never judge a book by its cover!
There are things you really should know.
She is not an animal lover!
She will bring destruction and woe!
Stay alert! Stay alive!
If she's coming your way, head east!
She'll give you the eye, as you go wand'ring by,
And if you're a wolf, you're deceased!
Stay alert! Stay alive!
If she's coming your way, head east!
She'll give you the eye, as you go wand'ring by,
And if you're a wolf, you're deceased!

(APPLAUSE)

19

Forward to
next track

SCENE CHANGE

The props for Red Riding Hood's house and the house of bricks are taken off-stage. If the children have composed music for the previous scene change, it could be played here too – see CD-ROM Music Activity.

SCENE 6 – The woodland

City type 1 steps foward.

CITY TYPE 1   A short while later, through the wood,
Came striding brave Miss Riding Hood.

Red Riding Hood enters from one side of the stage wearing her wolfskin coat. Wolf enters from the other side.

FARM ANIMAL 2   The Wolf stood there, his eyes ablaze,
And yellowish, like mayonnaise.

WOODLAND ANIMAL 2 His teeth were sharp, his gums were raw,
And spit was dripping from his jaw.

CITY TYPE 2   The maiden smiles. One eyelid flickers.
She draws a pistol from her knickers.
And bang! she hits the vital spot ...

CITY TYPE 2,
WOODLAND ANIMAL 2
AND FARM ANIMAL 2 And kills him with a single shot.

Red Riding Hood points a comic pistol at Wolf.

SOUND EFFECT – Gunshot

A gunshot is heard.

CHANT – Wolf dying

During the following chant, Wolf lurches about the stage until he finally falls dead at Red Riding Hood's feet.

ALL (EXCEPT WOLF) Blood dripping,
Bones cracking,
Life ebbing,
Wolf ... dying!
Blood dripping,
Bones cracking,
Life ebbing,
Wolf ... dying,
Wolf ... dying,
Wolf ... dying,
(descending bass line and final chord)
Dead!

Forward to next track

Wolf dies.

FARM ANIMAL 3 Pig, peeping through the window, stood
And yelled ...

PIG 3 "Well done, Miss Riding Hood!"

Everyone cheers as the song starts. Wolf's body is dragged off-stage during the first verse of the following song.

SONG – Done and dusted

ALL (EXCEPT RRH) Done and dusted,
Another job is done and dusted.
How lucky Mr Piggy trusted
Miss Riding Hood to
Come and slay the wolf!
Time to party,
Time to celebrate,
Time to have some fun.
Can't help feeling
It's a pity that we lost Pig Two
And we lost Pig One!

Solved and sorted,
This problem has been
Solved and sorted.
We think that it should be reported
Miss Riding Hood has once more saved the day!
She's a tonic,
She's supersonic!
Pig-defender and friend.
And thanks to her we'll have
A happy end.

21

There is a short instrumental break during which the photographer appears and snaps three photos of Red Riding Hood, Pig Three and the crowd.

Red Riding Hood exits arm-in-arm with Pig Three as the other animals wave goodbye.

ALL (EXCEPT RRH AND PIG 3)

Now and always,
They're friends forever.
Now and always,
It looks as though in
Big and small ways,
They'll be the best of mates
Through thick and thin.
Hand in trotter,
It seems they've gotta
Rosy future ahead.
Let's hear it for the Pig and Little Red!

(APPLAUSE)

SOUND EFFECT – Gunshot

A gunshot is heard from off-stage.

Everyone looks towards the noise and freezes in horror for a moment. Red Riding Hood enters wearing her wolfskin coat and carrying a travelling case. She speaks in a posh voice.

RED RIDING HOOD

Ah, Piglet, you must never trust
Young ladies from the upper crust.

CITY TYPE 1

For now, Miss Riding Hood, one notes,
Not only has two wolfskin coats,
But when she goes from place to place ...

ALL

She has a pigskin travelling case!

The whole cast returns to the stage for the final song.

SONG – Finale

(Reprise of Snouts and curly tails)

ALL

Now listen, ev'rybody!
And thanks for your attention,
But just before we end the show,
There's something we should mention.
We hope we made you chuckle and
We hope you got the gist,
We hope you sang along and that
You cheered and booed and hissed.
We hope you weren't offended
By the Roald Dahl twist.
But if you were, well ...

(What did you expect?)
What did you expect?
The usual ending?
What did you expect?
A work of art?
What did you expect?
The same old story?
The one where you can tell the ending
Right from the start?
Yes, what did you expect?
A Hollywood epic?
What did you expect?
A pantomime?
What did you expect?
A bedtime story?
Or would you rather relish
A Revolting Rhyme?

(Reprise of Done and dusted)

ALL   Tried and tested,
This story has been
Tried and tested.
Let's hope it kept you
Interested
And left you with a
Smile upon your face.
Don't be rotters,
Now raise your trotters, *(the children raise their hands ready to clap)*
Don't you know that you should? *(clap, clap)*

Let's hear it for the Pigs ...
One! Two! Three!
Let's hear it for the Wolf!
Boo! Hiss!
Let's hear it for the girl!
Hooray!
Red Riding Hood.

(APPLAUSE)

The entire cast takes a bow, gestures to the pianist or band, and then bows once more.

THE END

23

ALL (EXCEPT WOLF):

Chorus Well I ne - ver! What a cu - ri - ous sight, __ A

hun - gry wolf and a ne - ver - end - ing ap - pe - tite! He's a bul - ly, he's a

ra - ve - nous beast! __ But he saves a lit - tle some - thing, __ A tempt - ing lit - tle some - thing, __ A

tan - ta - lis - ing some - thing from his tas - ty __ feast. __

Huff and puff 2

Getting louder and faster throughout ♩· = 70

mp *mf*

I'll huff and I'll puff and I'll blow your house in, I'll

huff and I'll puff and I'll blow your house in, I'll huff and I'll puff and I'll blow your house in!

5

9 **accel.** *(The house is blown down.)*

Blowing sound effects

sub. ***p*** *cresc.*

Never-ending appetite (reprise)

With a swing ♩. = 120

ALL (EXCEPT WOLF):

Well I ne - ver! What a cu - ri - ous sight,___ A

hun - gry wolf and a ne - ver - end - ing ap - pe - tite!

He's a bul - ly, he's a ra - ve - nous beast!___ But he

saves a lit - tle some - thing,___ A tempt - ing lit - tle some - thing....___ A

tan - ta - lis - ing some - thing from his tas - ty___ feast.___

Wheeler-dealer piggy

Huff and puff 3

Getting louder and faster throughout ♩. = 70

I'll huff and I'll puff and I'll

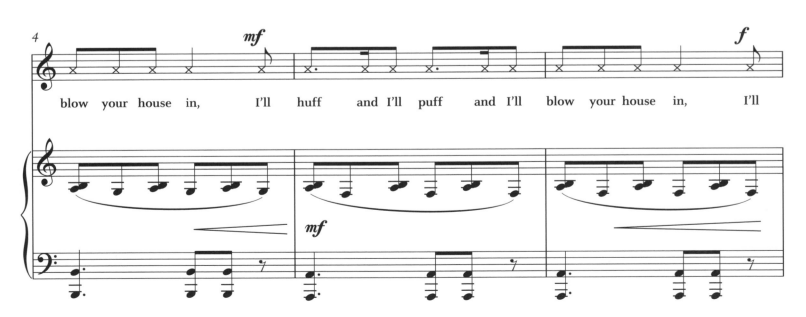

blow your house in, I'll huff and I'll puff and I'll blow your house in, I'll

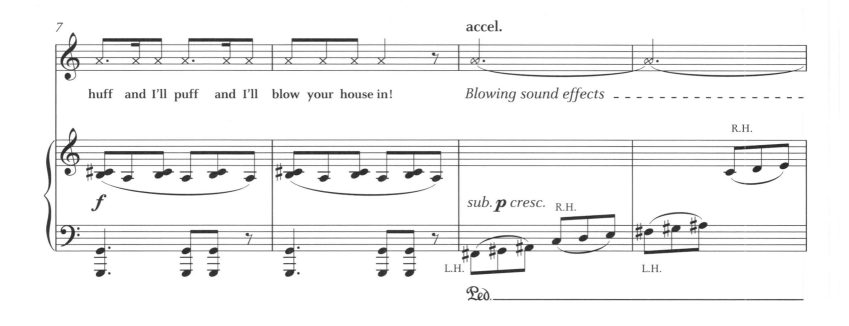

huff and I'll puff and I'll blow your house in! *Blowing sound effects* - - - - - - - - - - - - - - -

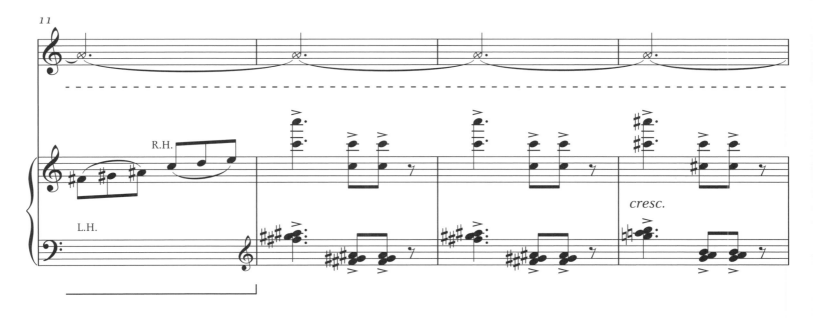

(Wolf, defeated, stops blowing.)

Perfectly marvellous me!

Sweetly ♩. = 54 RED RIDING HOOD: *mp*

Look in the mir - ror, What do I see?

Lit - tle me!
Quite ir - re - sis - ti - ble!

Gor - geous and lov - a - ble, Curls in my hair As
Sun - ny and sweet And

cute as can be,
kind as can be,

Per - fect - ly mar - vel - lous me! BUT!

ALL (EXCEPT RRH): ♪ = ♩
With a sense of urgency

mf

Wolf dying

With an air of suspense ♩. = 60

ALL (EXCEPT WOLF):

Blood drip-ping, Bones crack-ing,

Life ebb-ing, Wolf... dy-ing! Wolf... dy-ing,

Wolf... dy-ing, Wolf... dy-ing, Dead!

Done and dusted

Celebratory ♩. = 128

ALL (EXCEPT RRH): *f*

Done and dust-ed,____

An - o - ther job is done and dust - ed.____ How luck - y Mis - ter

D. S. 𝄋 to ⊕ then to Coda

⊕ CODA

Ro - sy fu - ture a - head.   Let's   hear   it   for   the Pig

and   Lit - tle___ Red!___

R.H.

CUE:	SINGERS:
	ALL

Finale

(Reprise of *Snouts and curly tails*)

Declamatory ♩ = 120   ALL: *f*

Now, lis-ten ev-'ry bo - dy, And thanks for your at-ten-tion, But just be-fore we end the show, There's some-thing we should men - tion. We hope we made you chuck-le and We

Don't be rot-ters,___ Now raise your trot-ters, – Don't you know that you

should? (clap) (clap) Let's hear it for the Pigs... One! Two! Three! Let's

hear it for the Wolf! Boo! Hiss! Let's hear it for the girl! Hoo -

ray! Red Ri - ding Hood.

R.H.

Applying for a performance licence at www.acblack.com/musicals

To present a public performance of one of our musicals you need a performance licence. We have created a simple and affordable system for buying licences online. Please visit www.acblack.com/musicals to apply online for a licence to perform this musical.

Here are some frequently asked questions about licensing:

What is a public performance?

A public performance – whether admission is charged or is free – is defined as a performance to an audience which includes any of the following: parents, relatives, friends, anyone who is not a member of the educational establishment performing the work.

What is a private performance?

If an audience is comprised solely of staff and pupils of the educational establishment performing the work, the performance is PRIVATE and you do not require a performance licence.

What does a performance licence let me do?

The performance licence allows you to present a public performance to a paying or non-paying audience within a one year time-period (the e-mail receipt we send you will be dated). Within that time period you may present one or more performances of the work and collect box office takings to a maximum of £500.

What am I allowed to photocopy if I have a performance licence?

A performance licence allows you to photocopy the printed script and CD-ROM text of the musical for rehearsal purposes. These copies should be destroyed after the musical for which they were licensed has been performed. A licence DOES NOT allow you to photocopy any other part of the musical. No part of any musical should be photocopied unless specifically permitted either by licence or by an exemption included in the individual musical.

What is a photocopy licence?

If you are intending to put on a private performance of a musical and you wish to make photocopies as above for this purpose, you may purchase a photocopy licence at a reduced fee.

What does a licence cost?

To find out the current cost of a photocopy or performance licence, please go to our website at www.acblack.com/musicals.

What about if I wish to video or record a performance?

If your school wishes to video or record a performance, either for your own internal use or in order to sell copies to parents, you must write to us separately to obtain permission. For videos or CDs sold we will issue you with an appropriate licence on payment of a percentage fee, calculated on the retail selling price and total number of copies produced. See below for our contact details.

What do I do if I can't pay online?

The online licensing scheme is quick and simple. We strongly urge you to use the scheme and to pay by credit/debit card if at all possible. We know that some schools may need to pay by other means, and we have a limited system for doing this. Please write to the address below, allowing one month's notice before the first performance date, and giving full contact details including telephone and email to:

The Copyright Manager,
Music Department,
A&C Black,
38 Soho Square,
London,
W1D 3HB.

Who benefits from the proceeds of licensing?

The writers! These are the talented people who put in long hard hours and wonderful creativity to produce great shows for schools to perform. The proceeds from your licence fees and the share of the box office takings are divided amongst them.

Licence fees also benefit The Roald Dahl Foundation – see page 40 for information about the Foundation's work.

Acknowledgements

First published 2007
by A&C Black Publishers Ltd
38 Soho Square, London, W1D 3HB.
© 2007 A&C Black Publishers Ltd
ISBN: 978 07136 8202 1

Text of The Three Little Pigs © 1982 Roald Dahl Nominee Ltd, reproduced by kind permission of Jonathan Cape & Puffin Books, and Alfred A. Knopf Inc.

Original lyrics, stage directions and drama activities for Roald Dahl's The Three Little Pigs © 2007 Matthew White

Original songs, musical arrangements and musical activities for Roald Dahl's The Three Little Pigs © 2007 Ana Sanderson

Original orchestral music for The Three Little Pigs by Paul Patterson © 2003 Josef Weinberger Ltd. Reproduced by kind permission.

Original orchestral music for The Three Little Pigs by Paul Patterson recorded by the London Philharmonic Orchestra conducted by David Parry.
© 2006 London Philharmonic Orchestra Ltd.

Inside illustrations © Moira Munro 2007
www.moiramunro.com

Cover illustrations © Quentin Blake 1982, 1997. Permission to use the illustrations by Quentin Blake in the book and accompanying CD-ROM is granted by AP Watt on behalf of Quentin Blake.

Edited by Harriet Lowe
Designed by Jocelyn Lucas and Tania Demidova
Music set by Jeanne Roberts

Songs performed by:
Matthew White and Sam Shaw (voices), David Fuest (clarinet) and John Whitfield (bassoon)

Recorded arrangements, sound engineering and mastering by Missak Takoushian. Vocals and live instruments recorded by Stephen Chadwick at 3D Music Ltd.

Enhanced CD post-production by Ian Shepherd and Karen Manning at Sound Recording Technology

Printed in Great Britain by Martins the Printers, Berwick-upon-Tweed

This book is produced using paper that is made from wood grown in managed, sustainable forests. It is natural, renewable and recyclable. The logging and manufacturing processes conform to the environmental regulations of the country of origin.

The publishers and authors would like to thank the many children, teachers and schools who helped in the preparation of Roald Dahl's The Three Little Pigs. In particular we thank: Debbie Woo and the staff and children of Winhills Primary School, St Neots; Hilary Hill and the staff and children of Turvey Lower School, Bedford; Laura Stevens and the staff and children of Kingswood Primary School, London; Valerie Bannan, Margaret Taylor and the staff and children of Claires Court School, The College, Maidenhead; and Kath Sayer and the staff and children of Towers Junior School, Hornchurch.

We are also very grateful for the enthusiasm and support given by the Roald Dahl Foundation and their representatives: Amanda Conquy, Liccy Dahl, Anthony Goff, Georgia Glover and Donald Sturrock.

The making of a musical – a Revolting start

The Three Little Pigs is one of Roald Dahl's enormously popular *Revolting Rhymes*. In it, Piggy Number Three calls on Red Riding Hood to save him from the ever-hungry Wolf, which she duly does – but little does Piggy realise that she fancies a pigskin handbag to go with her new wolfskin coat ...

A&C Black has already published other hugely popular adaptations of Roald Dahl's *Revolting Rhymes*: **Snow-White and the Seven Dwarfs**, **Jack and the Beanstalk**, **Little Red Riding Hood and the Wolf** and **Goldilocks and the Three Bears**. Now the story of the three little pigs can also be enjoyed as a musical for children to perform. How these adaptations have come about is an interesting story in itself.

To benefit the Roald Dahl Foundation, several major orchestral works based on Roald Dahl's stories and rhymes have been commissioned. Written by some of the greatest living composers, they have been performed to huge audiences of children around the world. The orchestral music for **The Three Little Pigs** was written by Paul Patterson and was first performed in Basel in 2004 by the Basel Symphony Orchestra. It has since been performed worldwide and was recently recorded by the London Philharmonic Orchestra at the Queen Elizabeth Hall, London, in 2006.

It is the aim of Felicity Dahl (Roald Dahl's widow) and of the Roald Dahl Foundation to take the music even closer to the lives of children. The aim of this musical adaptation of **The Three Little Pigs** is to give children the opportunity to perform the story themselves. Roald Dahl's rhyme forms the script of the musical, which is interwoven with a set of songs to perform, many of which contain themes and motifs from Paul Patterson's orchestral work. On the CD there is a selection of extracts from the orchestral work to underpin mime, dramatic action and dance.

About the Roald Dahl Foundation

The Roald Dahl Foundation offers a programme of grant-giving to charities, hospitals and individuals in the UK. The help delivered by the Foundation spreads far and wide. It supports people in exactly the same way Roald Dahl did when he was alive, offering practical assistance to children and families in its three areas of interest: neurology, haematology and literacy.

Funded partly through its original endowment, the Foundation also benefits from a range of fundraising activities, most notably the national sponsored event, Readathon (www.readathon.org). In addition, the Wondercrump Friends of the Foundation arrange a programme of local events and many schoolchildren fundraise on its behalf. Since its creation in 1991, the Foundation has donated over £5 million in grants.

Visit roalddahl.com

The Roald Dahl website is an innovative and large site, bursting with content that will appeal to a wide range of key audiences – child and adult, parent, teacher and librarian – around the globe. It is packed with everything you ever wanted to know about Roald Dahl's life and work, with material ranging from a detailed biography and database of works, to an online club for kids, a growing resource of lesson ideas for teachers, and links to information about the Roald Dahl Foundation and the Roald Dahl Museum and Story Centre.

About the writers and composers

Matthew White is an experienced writer, director and actor, particularly in the field of musical theatre. Recent West End credits include directing **Little Shop of Horrors** and performing in **Chicago**, **The Phantom of the Opera**, **Ragtime** and **Les Misérables.** Other published works include a theatrical adaptation of **Far From the Madding Crowd** (Samuel French), **Staging a Musical** (A&C Black) and the musical adaptation for children of **Roald Dahl's Little Red Riding Hood and the Wolf** and **Roald Dahl's Jack and the Beanstalk** (A&C Black). Matthew lives in London with his wife, Lindsey, and two daughters, Lydia and Xanthe.

Ana Sanderson is a song-writer, composer and children's music editor. She wrote the music for the musical adaptation of **Roald Dahl's Little Red Riding Hood and the Wolf** and for **Roald Dahl's Jack and the Beanstalk** (A&C Black). As an editor, she worked on various publications including **Three Rapping Rats**, **Banana Splits** and **Recorder Magic**, and she continues to work on developing new musicals for children. She plays in a band with her husband Jason, and they live near Cambridge with their children, Edward and Nina.

Paul Patterson is one of the most successful English composers of his generation. His early works for wind instruments have become standard repertoire, he has composed much for film, and his large-scale choral works are performed widely in Britain and abroad. His setting of **Roald Dahl's Little Red Riding Hood** has been performed all over the world, recorded internationally, and filmed by the BBC. He has worked extensively in music education and was Head of Contemporary Music and Composition at the Royal Academy of Music for many years.

www.acblack.com/musicals

Visit **www.acblack.com/musicals** for a wealth of information about other musicals published by A&C Black (see opposite). You can also purchase a performance licence, listen to audio samples of songs from all the musicals, find out how to join the Musicals Hall of Fame and read about taking part in trialling a new A&C Black musical.